THIS *planner* BELONGS TO

SCHOOL

ROOM

GRADE

ADDRESS

EMAIL

PHONE

Contacts and Volunteers

NAME	CONTACT INFO

SCHEDULE

SCHOOL BEGINS: ______

LUNCH: ______

RECESS: ______

SPECIALS: ______

SCHOOL ENDS: ______

NEED HELP?

RELIABLE STUDENTS: ______

______

______

TEACHERS: ______

______

PRINCIPAL: ______

VICE PRINCIPAL: ______

______

OTHER STAFF: ______

______

SPECIAL SCHEDULES

NAME	TIME AND LOCATION	ADDITIONAL NOTES

COMMUNICATION LOG

DATE	TYPE	NAME	PURPOSE	NOTES

COMMUNICATION LOG

DATE	TYPE	NAME	PURPOSE	NOTES

NEWS AND NOTES

NEWS AND NOTES

PLAN IT

USE THESE PAGES TO CREATE A CLASSROOM PLAN, RECORD SEATING CHARTS, CREATE CHECKLISTS, SKETCH PLANS, ETC. THE OPTIONS ARE ENDLESS!

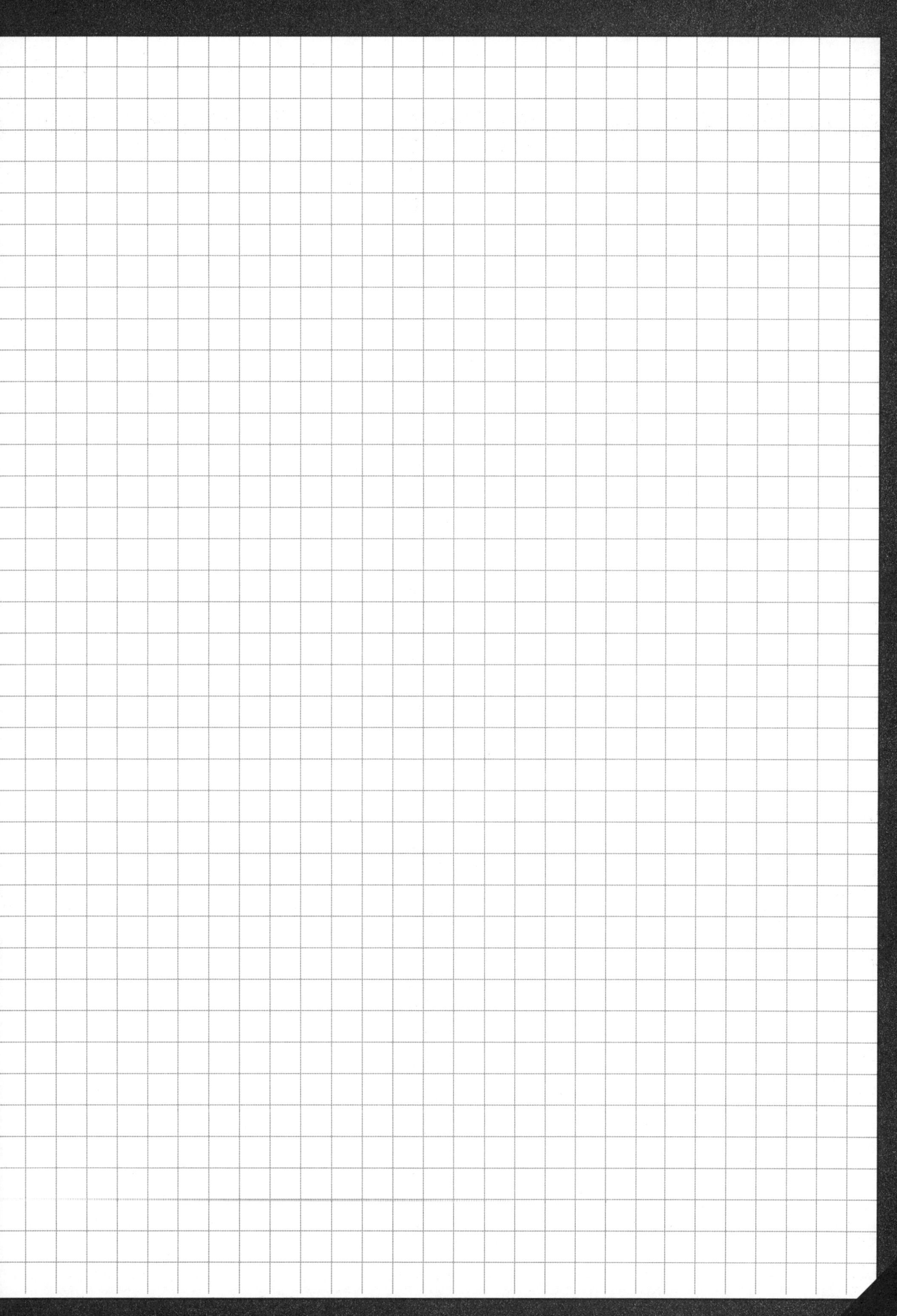

YEAR AT A *Glance*

JULY

AUGUST

SEPTEMBER

OCTOBER

NOVEMBER

DECEMBER

JANUARY
FEBRUARY
MARCH
APRIL
MAY
JUNE

JULY

SUNDAY	MONDAY	TUESDAY	WEDNESDAY

IMPORTANT DATES	GOALS

THURSDAY	FRIDAY	SATURDAY

HAVE TO DO

NOTES

PSST! USE THESE GUIDES TO KEEP YOUR TABS PERFECTLY PLACED.

AUGUST

The grass is greener where you are.

SUNDAY	MONDAY	TUESDAY	WEDNESDAY

IMPORTANT DATES

GOALS

THURSDAY	FRIDAY	SATURDAY

HAVE TO DO

NOTES

SEPTEMBER

Don't stop until you're proud.

SUNDAY	MONDAY	TUESDAY	WEDNESDAY

IMPORTANT DATES

GOALS

THURSDAY	FRIDAY	SATURDAY

HAVE TO DO

NOTES

OCTOBER

Take your dreams seriously.

SUNDAY	MONDAY	TUESDAY	WEDNESDAY

IMPORTANT DATES

GOALS

THURSDAY	FRIDAY	SATURDAY

HAVE TO DO

NOTES

NOVEMBER

Look for the helpers.

SUNDAY	MONDAY	TUESDAY	WEDNESDAY

IMPORTANT DATES

GOALS

THURSDAY	FRIDAY	SATURDAY

HAVE TO DO

NOTES

DECEMBER

We may bloom differently, but in this class we grow together.

SUNDAY	MONDAY	TUESDAY	WEDNESDAY

IMPORTANT DATES

GOALS

THURSDAY	FRIDAY	SATURDAY

HAVE TO DO

NOTES

JANUARY

Human. Kind. Be both.

SUNDAY	MONDAY	TUESDAY	WEDNESDAY

IMPORTANT DATES

GOALS

THURSDAY	FRIDAY	SATURDAY

HAVE TO DO

NOTES

FEBRUARY

Be proud of how hard you are trying.

SUNDAY	MONDAY	TUESDAY	WEDNESDAY

IMPORTANT DATES

GOALS

THURSDAY	FRIDAY	SATURDAY

HAVE TO DO

NOTES

MARCH

SUNDAY	MONDAY	TUESDAY	WEDNESDAY

IMPORTANT DATES

GOALS

THURSDAY	FRIDAY	SATURDAY

HAVE TO DO

NOTES

APRIL

Every day is a fresh start.

SUNDAY	MONDAY	TUESDAY	WEDNESDAY

IMPORTANT DATES

GOALS

THURSDAY	FRIDAY	SATURDAY

HAVE TO DO

NOTES

MAY

SUNDAY	MONDAY	TUESDAY	WEDNESDAY

IMPORTANT DATES

GOALS

THURSDAY	FRIDAY	SATURDAY

HAVE TO DO

NOTES

JUNE

No one is perfect. That's why pencils have erasers.

SUNDAY	MONDAY	TUESDAY	WEDNESDAY

IMPORTANT DATES

GOALS

THURSDAY	FRIDAY	SATURDAY

HAVE TO DO

NOTES

week #	SUBJECT	SUBJECT	SUBJECT
MONDAY			
TUESDAY			
WEDNESDAY			
THURSDAY			
FRIDAY			

SUBJECT	SUBJECT	SUBJECT	SUBJECT

PSST! CUT THIS CORNER OFF EACH WEEK TO MARK AND FIND YOUR PLACE EASILY.

week #	SUBJECT	SUBJECT	SUBJECT
MONDAY			
TUESDAY			
WEDNESDAY			
THURSDAY			
FRIDAY			

SUBJECT	SUBJECT	SUBJECT	SUBJECT

week #	SUBJECT	SUBJECT	SUBJECT
MONDAY			
TUESDAY			
WEDNESDAY			
THURSDAY			
FRIDAY			

SUBJECT	SUBJECT	SUBJECT	SUBJECT

week #	SUBJECT	SUBJECT	SUBJECT
MONDAY			
TUESDAY			
WEDNESDAY			
THURSDAY			
FRIDAY			

SUBJECT	SUBJECT	SUBJECT	SUBJECT

week #	SUBJECT	SUBJECT	SUBJECT
MONDAY			
TUESDAY			
WEDNESDAY			
THURSDAY			
FRIDAY			

SUBJECT	SUBJECT	SUBJECT	SUBJECT

week #	SUBJECT	SUBJECT	SUBJECT
MONDAY			
TUESDAY			
WEDNESDAY			
THURSDAY			
FRIDAY			

SUBJECT	SUBJECT	SUBJECT	SUBJECT

week #	SUBJECT	SUBJECT	SUBJECT
MONDAY			
TUESDAY			
WEDNESDAY			
THURSDAY			
FRIDAY			

SUBJECT	SUBJECT	SUBJECT	SUBJECT

week #	SUBJECT	SUBJECT	SUBJECT

MONDAY

TUESDAY

WEDNESDAY

THURSDAY

FRIDAY

SUBJECT	SUBJECT	SUBJECT	SUBJECT

week #	SUBJECT	SUBJECT	SUBJECT
MONDAY			
TUESDAY			
WEDNESDAY			
THURSDAY			
FRIDAY			

SUBJECT	SUBJECT	SUBJECT	SUBJECT

week #

	SUBJECT	SUBJECT	SUBJECT
MONDAY			
TUESDAY			
WEDNESDAY			
THURSDAY			
FRIDAY			

SUBJECT	SUBJECT	SUBJECT	SUBJECT

week #	SUBJECT	SUBJECT	SUBJECT
MONDAY			
TUESDAY			
WEDNESDAY			
THURSDAY			
FRIDAY			

SUBJECT	SUBJECT	SUBJECT	SUBJECT

week #	SUBJECT	SUBJECT	SUBJECT
MONDAY			
TUESDAY			
WEDNESDAY			
THURSDAY			
FRIDAY			

SUBJECT	SUBJECT	SUBJECT	SUBJECT

week #	SUBJECT	SUBJECT	SUBJECT
MONDAY			
TUESDAY			
WEDNESDAY			
THURSDAY			
FRIDAY			

SUBJECT	SUBJECT	SUBJECT	SUBJECT

week #	SUBJECT	SUBJECT	SUBJECT

MONDAY

TUESDAY

WEDNESDAY

THURSDAY

FRIDAY

SUBJECT	SUBJECT	SUBJECT	SUBJECT

week #	SUBJECT	SUBJECT	SUBJECT
MONDAY			
TUESDAY			
WEDNESDAY			
THURSDAY			
FRIDAY			

SUBJECT	SUBJECT	SUBJECT	SUBJECT

week #	SUBJECT	SUBJECT	SUBJECT
MONDAY			
TUESDAY			
WEDNESDAY			
THURSDAY			
FRIDAY			

SUBJECT	SUBJECT	SUBJECT	SUBJECT

week #	SUBJECT	SUBJECT	SUBJECT
MONDAY			
TUESDAY			
WEDNESDAY			
THURSDAY			
FRIDAY			

SUBJECT	SUBJECT	SUBJECT	SUBJECT

week #	SUBJECT	SUBJECT	SUBJECT
MONDAY			
TUESDAY			
WEDNESDAY			
THURSDAY			
FRIDAY			

SUBJECT	SUBJECT	SUBJECT	SUBJECT

week #	SUBJECT	SUBJECT	SUBJECT
MONDAY			
TUESDAY			
WEDNESDAY			
THURSDAY			
FRIDAY			

SUBJECT	SUBJECT	SUBJECT	SUBJECT

week #	SUBJECT	SUBJECT	SUBJECT
MONDAY			
TUESDAY			
WEDNESDAY			
THURSDAY			
FRIDAY			

SUBJECT	SUBJECT	SUBJECT	SUBJECT

week #	SUBJECT	SUBJECT	SUBJECT
MONDAY			
TUESDAY			
WEDNESDAY			
THURSDAY			
FRIDAY			

SUBJECT	SUBJECT	SUBJECT	SUBJECT

week #	SUBJECT	SUBJECT	SUBJECT
MONDAY			
TUESDAY			
WEDNESDAY			
THURSDAY			
FRIDAY			

SUBJECT	SUBJECT	SUBJECT	SUBJECT

week #

SUBJECT	SUBJECT	SUBJECT

MONDAY

TUESDAY

WEDNESDAY

THURSDAY

FRIDAY

SUBJECT	SUBJECT	SUBJECT	SUBJECT

week #	SUBJECT	SUBJECT	SUBJECT
MONDAY			
TUESDAY			
WEDNESDAY			
THURSDAY			
FRIDAY			

SUBJECT	SUBJECT	SUBJECT	SUBJECT

week #	SUBJECT	SUBJECT	SUBJECT
MONDAY			
TUESDAY			
WEDNESDAY			
THURSDAY			
FRIDAY			

SUBJECT	SUBJECT	SUBJECT	SUBJECT

week #	SUBJECT	SUBJECT	SUBJECT
MONDAY			
TUESDAY			
WEDNESDAY			
THURSDAY			
FRIDAY			

SUBJECT	SUBJECT	SUBJECT	SUBJECT

week #	SUBJECT	SUBJECT	SUBJECT
MONDAY			
TUESDAY			
WEDNESDAY			
THURSDAY			
FRIDAY			

SUBJECT	SUBJECT	SUBJECT	SUBJECT

week #	SUBJECT	SUBJECT	SUBJECT
MONDAY			
TUESDAY			
WEDNESDAY			
THURSDAY			
FRIDAY			

SUBJECT	SUBJECT	SUBJECT	SUBJECT

week #	SUBJECT	SUBJECT	SUBJECT

MONDAY			
TUESDAY			
WEDNESDAY			
THURSDAY			
FRIDAY			

SUBJECT	SUBJECT	SUBJECT	SUBJECT

week #	SUBJECT	SUBJECT	SUBJECT
MONDAY			
TUESDAY			
WEDNESDAY			
THURSDAY			
FRIDAY			

SUBJECT	SUBJECT	SUBJECT	SUBJECT

week #

SUBJECT	SUBJECT	SUBJECT

MONDAY

TUESDAY

WEDNESDAY

THURSDAY

FRIDAY

SUBJECT	SUBJECT	SUBJECT	SUBJECT

week #	SUBJECT	SUBJECT	SUBJECT
MONDAY			
TUESDAY			
WEDNESDAY			
THURSDAY			
FRIDAY			

SUBJECT	SUBJECT	SUBJECT	SUBJECT

week #	SUBJECT	SUBJECT	SUBJECT
MONDAY			
TUESDAY			
WEDNESDAY			
THURSDAY			
FRIDAY			

SUBJECT	SUBJECT	SUBJECT	SUBJECT

week #	SUBJECT	SUBJECT	SUBJECT
MONDAY			
TUESDAY			
WEDNESDAY			
THURSDAY			
FRIDAY			

SUBJECT	SUBJECT	SUBJECT	SUBJECT

week #	SUBJECT	SUBJECT	SUBJECT
MONDAY			
TUESDAY			
WEDNESDAY			
THURSDAY			
FRIDAY			

SUBJECT	SUBJECT	SUBJECT	SUBJECT

week #	SUBJECT	SUBJECT	SUBJECT
MONDAY			
TUESDAY			
WEDNESDAY			
THURSDAY			
FRIDAY			

SUBJECT	SUBJECT	SUBJECT	SUBJECT

week #	SUBJECT	SUBJECT	SUBJECT
MONDAY			
TUESDAY			
WEDNESDAY			
THURSDAY			
FRIDAY			

SUBJECT	SUBJECT	SUBJECT	SUBJECT

week #	SUBJECT	SUBJECT	SUBJECT
MONDAY			
TUESDAY			
WEDNESDAY			
THURSDAY			
FRIDAY			

SUBJECT	SUBJECT	SUBJECT	SUBJECT

week #	SUBJECT	SUBJECT	SUBJECT
MONDAY			
TUESDAY			
WEDNESDAY			
THURSDAY			
FRIDAY			

SUBJECT	SUBJECT	SUBJECT	SUBJECT

week #	SUBJECT	SUBJECT	SUBJECT
MONDAY			
TUESDAY			
WEDNESDAY			
THURSDAY			
FRIDAY			

SUBJECT	SUBJECT	SUBJECT	SUBJECT

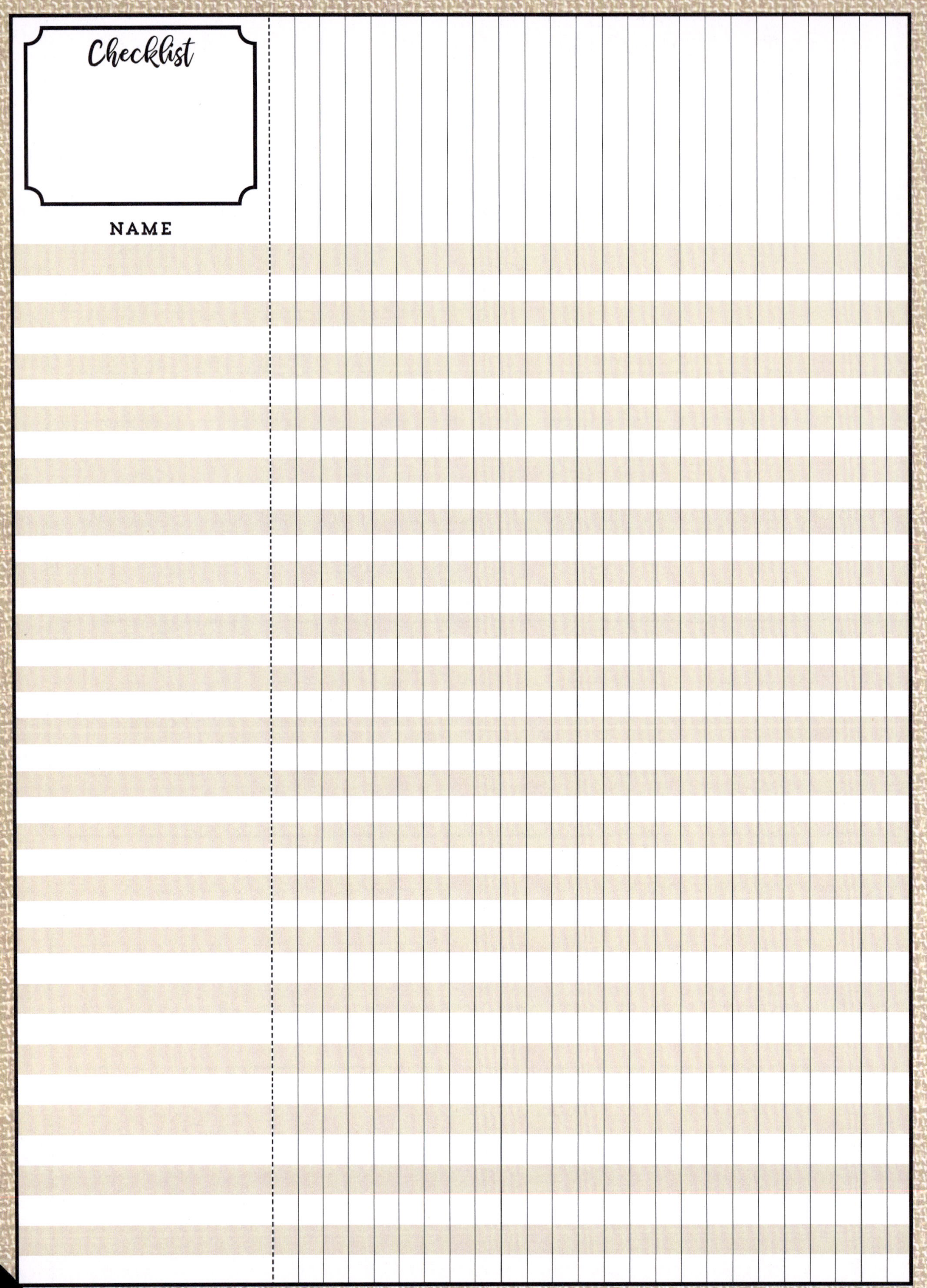

Checklist
NAME

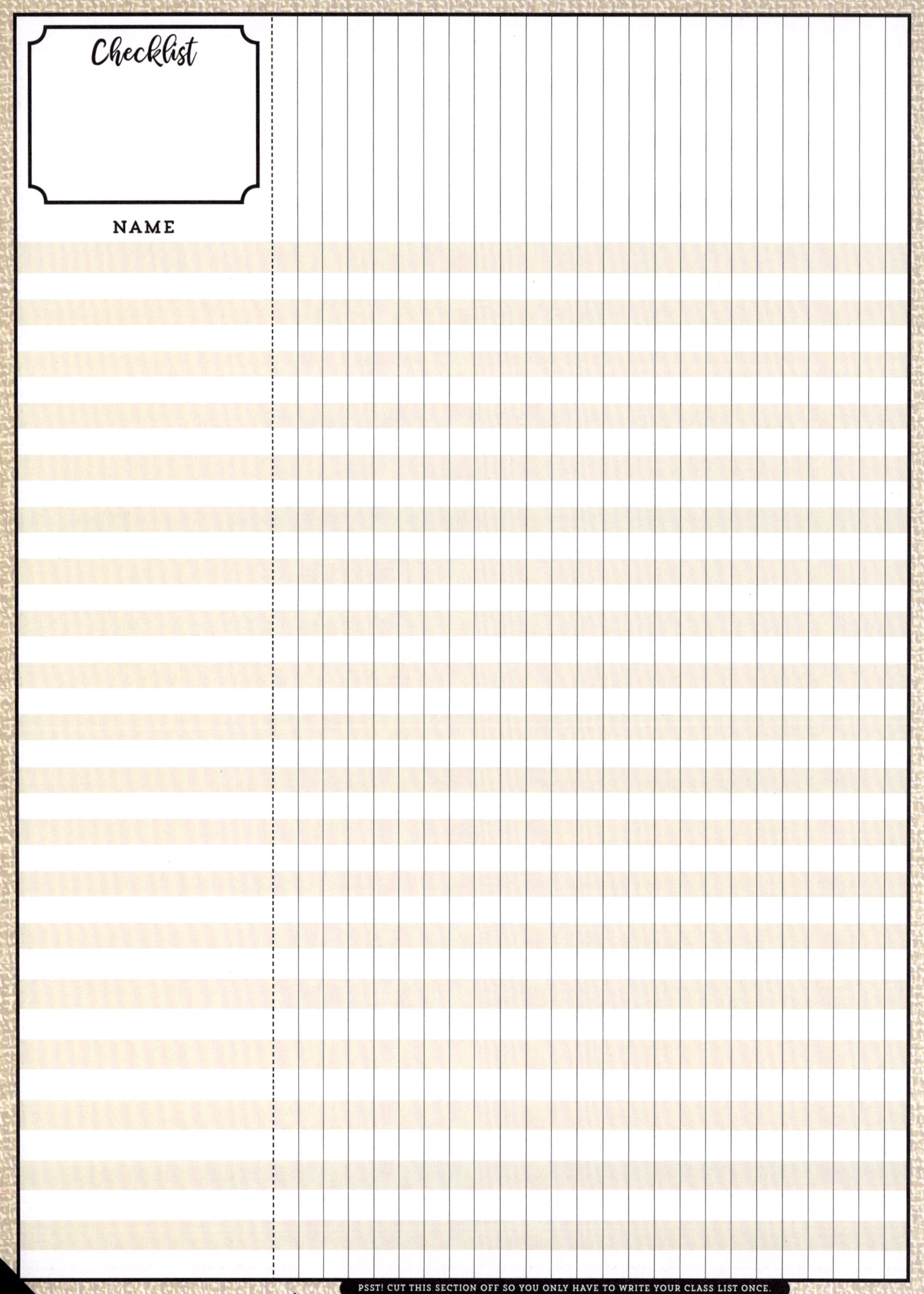

PSST! CUT THIS SECTION OFF SO YOU ONLY HAVE TO WRITE YOUR CLASS LIST ONCE.

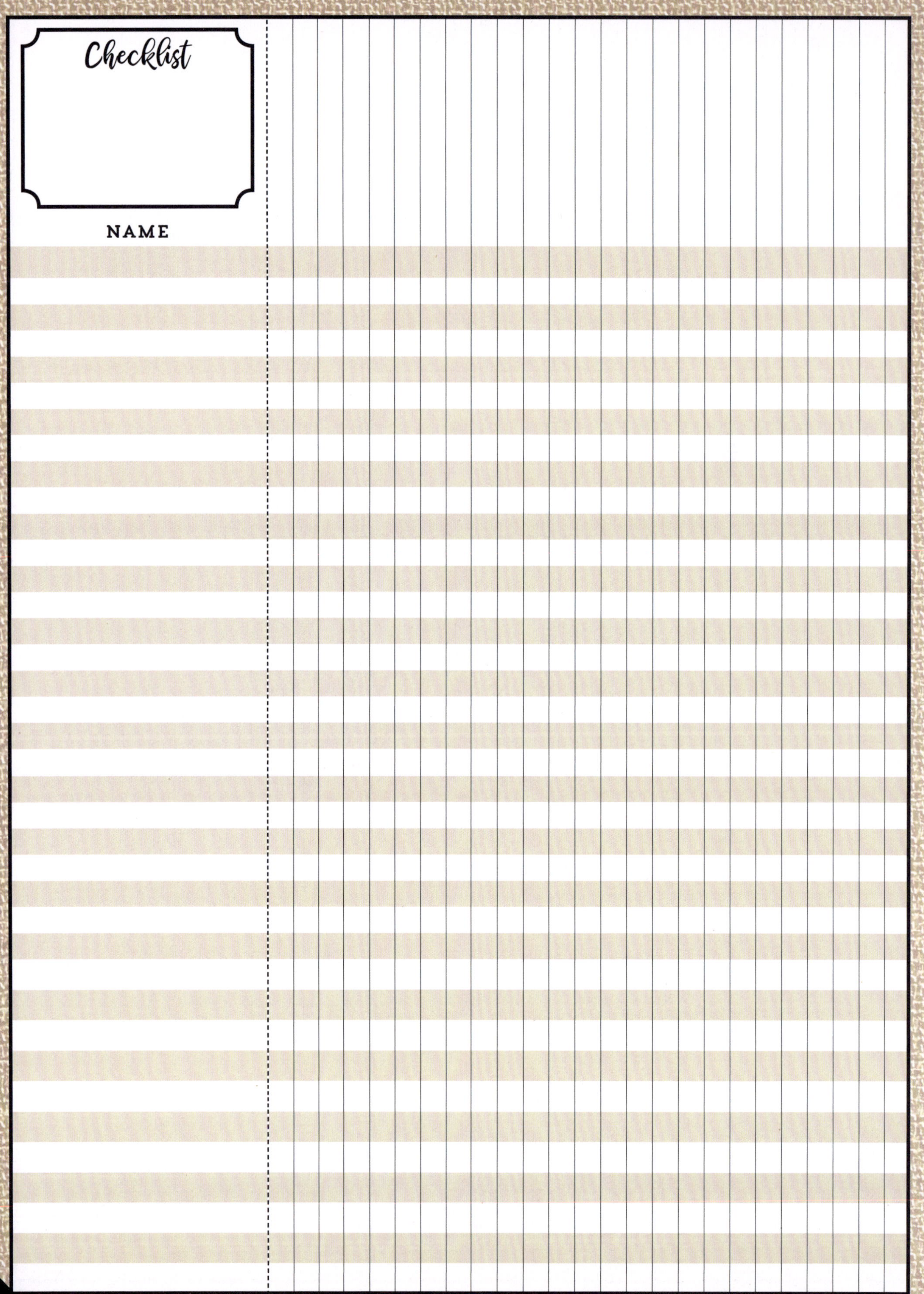
Checklist
NAME

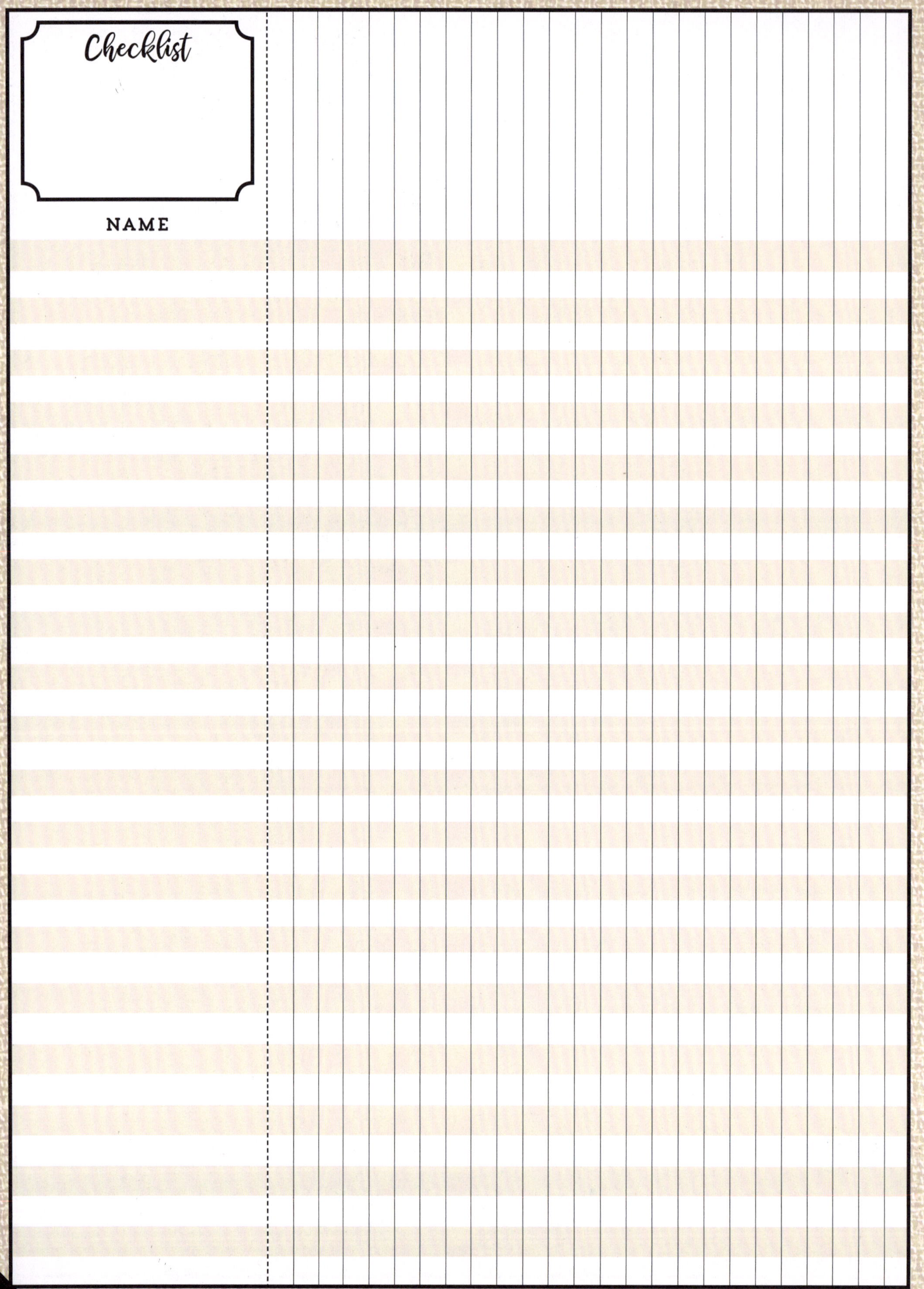
Checklist
NAME

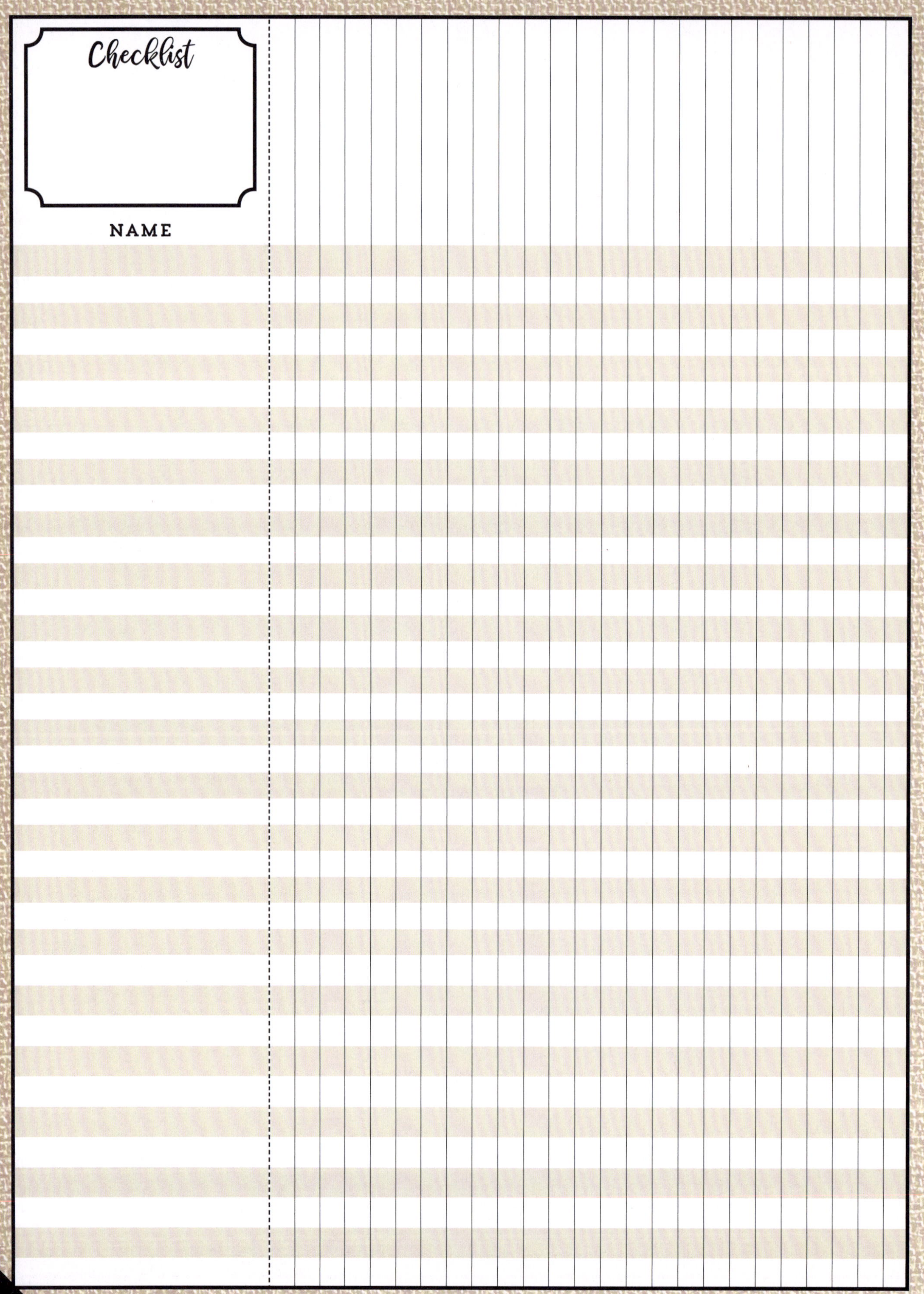
Checklist
NAME

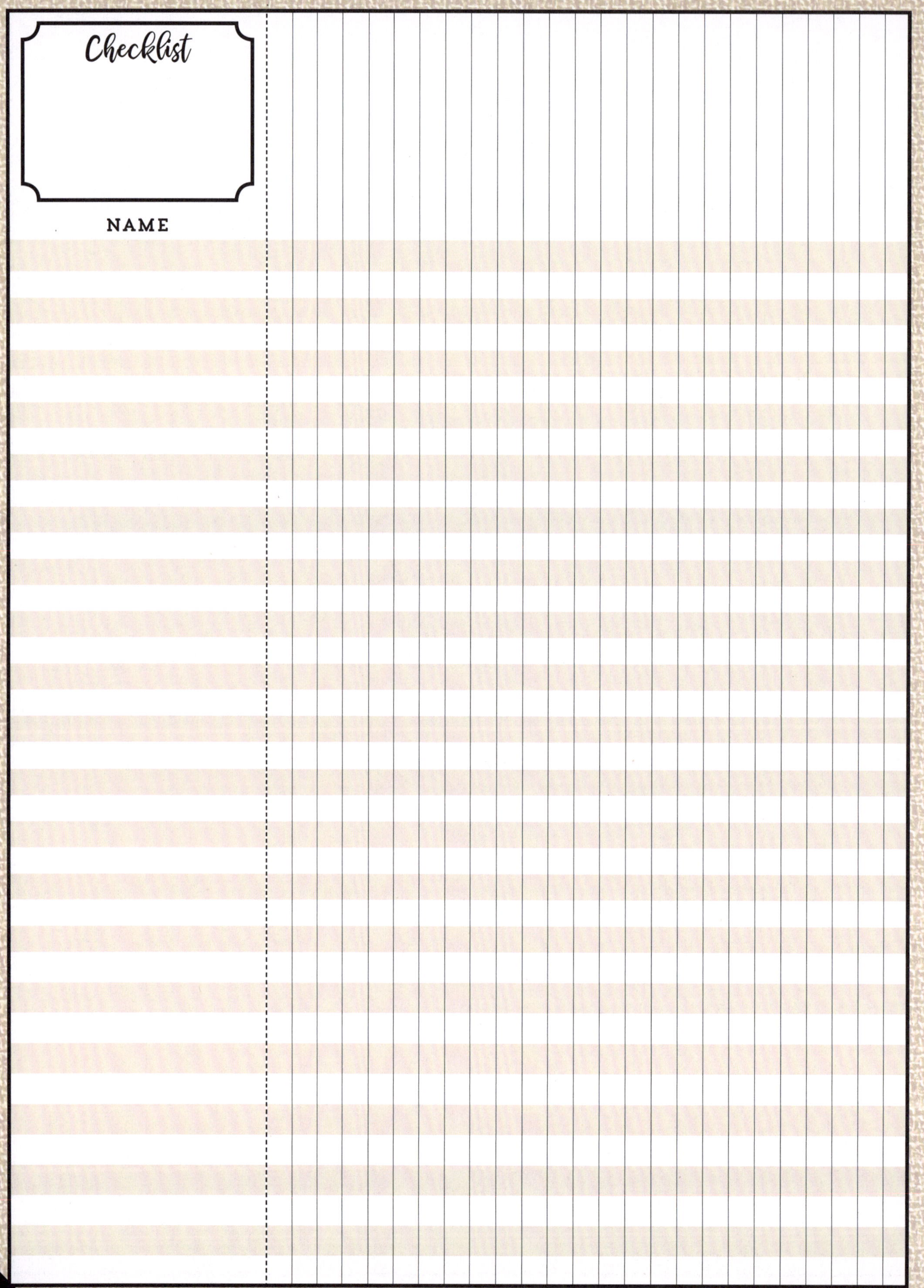
Checklist
NAME

TEACHERS
ARE LIKE
great books.

EVERYONE CAN

NAME ONE THAT

changed

THEIR LIFE.

OCTOBER
OCTOBER

FEBRUARY
FEBRUARY

JUNE
JUNE

LESSON PLANS
LESSON PLANS

SEPTEMBER
SEPTEMBER

JANUARY
JANUARY

MAY
MAY

CHECKLISTS
CHECKLISTS

AUGUST
AUGUST

DECEMBER
DECEMBER

APRIL
APRIL

JULY
JULY

NOVEMBER
NOVEMBER

MARCH
MARCH